Left-Handed Poetry

poems by

Linda Lamenza

Finishing Line Press
Georgetown, Kentucky

Left-Handed Poetry

Copyright © 2024 by Linda Lamenza
ISBN 979-8-88838-525-8 First Edition
All rights reserved under International and Pan-American Copyright Conventions. No part of this book may be reproduced in any manner whatsoever without written permission from the publisher, except in the case of brief quotations embodied in critical articles and reviews.

ACKNOWLEDGMENTS

I am grateful to the editors of the following journals/books in which these poems first appeared, in some cases, in another form:

Tishman Review, October 2017, vol. 3, issue 4: "Pumpkin Picking"
Main Street Rag, Fall 2019, vol. 24 #4: "Ambulance: Daydream:"
Rogue Agent, Nov. 2019, Issue 56: "Atomic number 22: Titanium"
Ovunque Siamo, September, 2020, "Left-Handed Poetry," "Absently She Mutters, How's Your Arm?"
The Healing Muse, October 21, 2020, vol. 20.: "They arrive at the ER," and "After four months, I can take a walk"
Nixes Mate Anthology, In the Time of Covid, 2021: "Oxy"

Publisher: Leah Huete de Maines
Editor: Christen Kincaid
Cover Art: Linda Lamenza
Author Photo: Kristina Watts
Cover Design: Elizabeth Maines McCleavy

Order online: www.finishinglinepress.com
also available on amazon.com

Author inquiries and mail orders:
Finishing Line Press
PO Box 1626
Georgetown, Kentucky 40324
USA

Contents

On Rainbows 1
Honda Pilot 2
On The Asphalt 3
Ambulance: Daydream 4
Sunset in the Emergency Room 5
Diagnosis: Wrecked 6
They Arrive at the ER, ... 7
Just Like So Many Other Things 8
Absently She Mutters, How's Your Arm? 9
Watching The Palio di Siena on the Hospital TV 10
Left-Handed Poetry 11
Atomic Number 22: Titanium 13
A Month in the Rehab Unit 14
The Summer that Wasn't 15
Oxy 16
Another Ambulance Daydream 17
Date Night 18
The Damned Splint 19
7:40 A.M. on a Weekday 20
Ode to the Commode 21
The Baltimore Therapeutic Equipment Work Simulator ... 22
Intake Interview: The Ride 23
Breakdown at CVS 24
Pumpkin-picking Festival: Concord, Mass 25
I Miss My Daughter's First Year of Middle School 26
Four Months Later: I walk again 27
Back to Work 28
Four Years to the Day 29
Right of Way 30

"Hope" is the thing with feathers – Emily Dickinson

For every one of my family and friends, who went through this accident and its aftermath with me.

In memory of Madeline S. McEneney, 1969-2020.

On Rainbows

To see one
you must turn
your back
to the sun,
there must be rain
in another part of the sky,
each drop lit
by the sun's white menu.
And a secondary
luminosity trapped
inside the rain,
twice reflected,
reversing order:
Violet Indigo
Blue Green
Yellow Orange
Red—
an ordinary rainbow,
memorized
in primary school.
To miss it
your back
must be flat
on the hospital bed,
curtains drawn,
outside world
notwithstanding.

Honda Pilot

Truth is the purple swollen
disaster of my foot,

where her tire wrecked me
in the Mobil parking lot.

My right elbow
a shattered bone I can

no longer lean on.
Now, I'm a part of her

SUV,
my DNA

forever embedded
in her bumper.

On the Asphalt

From my mind I draw a card: Courage,
cross the Ponte Vecchio,
toss into the Arno my pain.
They're all here:
the Mobil station manager,
the sisters who got out of their
car to help me.
I'm off to sip cappuccino
at Bar Ortensia.
Empty my pockets,
make room for joy
like tourists in the Uffizi courtyard
who pose next to the twin
of Michelangelo's David.
Both of us could pass for real.

Ambulance: Daydream

Surrender
to motion, be
carried by strangers.
Back-float on the sea.

Feel the burning sand
my broken foot,
my elbow, seaweed.
Hooks that hold bottles
are clouds above,
my good arm shields my eyes
from the fake sun.

Ambulance wheels are sandpipers skittering
the threshold,

the glistening IV bag,
jellyfish that looms.

The monitor that beeps:
a laughing gull.

Sunset in the Emergency Room

My reflection fades from the stainless-steel IV pole,
wet with tears.
They wheel me on a gurney,
ask my name and birthdate,
but I don't know.
My body's covered in a blanket
that sears my skin and limbs.
I know I'm in trouble,
staring at the ceiling
waiting for anyone to tell me
who I am.

Diagnosis: Wrecked

The curse is the mark,
like Alpine Swiss,
across my fifth metatarsal.
Sometimes it's a map,
or Monet's *Water Lilies*
in deep reds and pinks,
wrecked by someone's SUV,
a ghoulish work of art
by Saturday's driver.

They Arrive at the ER,

each of them separately,
spaced apart by minutes,
like thoughts.

My sister murmurs *Lin, Lin*
my brother cringes
at the sight of me,

my love
smooths her hand on my forehead.
They try not to gasp at the cervical collar,

the stiff plastic cage
that holds me.
Mangled arm,

swollen purple foot.
They sit in chairs in one row, across from
my bed, binge-watching me like Netflix.

Just Like So Many Other Things

1.

Alone in the hospital bathroom
I steady myself,
eyes closed, not a white
Johnny, but the wedding
gown I wish I'd worn,
not the non-slip socks,
not the call button.

2.

The architectural hum of my vitals cannot hide.
Though they've "lit" a faux vanilla candle
in the community craft room
beside Travel & Leisure—
play soft music,
there's no way to make this pretty.

3.
The air conditioner rattles the light fixture,
blows hard against the curtain around my bed.
I follow the Physical Therapist
to the small room,
balance fear on the edge of the sink.
This may hurt, she says.

Absently She Mutters, How's Your Arm?

My mother sits motionless
except her lips
which move in prayer.
She tells the old stories in Italian:
dusty wine bottles
in the cave under the bottega
during the air raid,
the sirens whining.
My eight-year-old mother running
atraverso gli uliveti,
skirt flying like the parachute
she chases, until it lands
and she catches up with it.

Watching The Palio di Siena on the Hospital TV

After a Tide commercial,
horses arrive in the cathedral,
horseshoes tapping on marble,
horseheads adorned with dyed bridles,
stallions, all of them, majestic beside their riders
matching vests, angeled frescoes,
each receiving his blessing
from the carmine-cassocked priest:
go, go and return victorious.

Piazza del Campo
A sea of sap-green hats, gold capes, shields, Revelers swarm
the riders and horses
'round the treacherous shell-shaped course.
Three hours of pageantry;
the flags, ancient anthems croon.
Drums and hooves against wind.

Left-Handed Poetry

Two weeks post-surgery
episode of *Breaking
Bad* briefly holds

my attention, extra large
cucumber shows
up in the garden,

my sister gives
me a shimmering
tattoo of a mermaid,

in honor of her birthday.
Oliver Sacks dies
on August 30th,

while I am reading
his biography.
I create a plan

for the first day of school,
though I won't be teaching.
I pretend to go

see the new Mission
Impossible movie:
Rogue Nation.

Dog retrieves
his lost chew-toy
from under the sofa.

I FaceTime
with Madeline,
compare pains

and past-times.
While the ink-black
scab on my elbow

flakes off,
I practice printing
with my left hand.

Atomic Number 22: Titanium

From the Greek word titans,
used in the aerospace industry—
airframes, engines,
screw blades on ships,
bike frames that withstand extreme
temperatures.
Strong as steel, only lighter.
Found in meteorites and the sun,
only element that burns in pure
nitrogen.
High strength, toughness,
corrosion resistant
wedding rings,
low-density money clips,
artists' paints, my
reconstructed elbow.

A Month in the Rehab Unit

I am shattered
into no particular
order like bits of colored glass
on the stone floor.

Let my selves
come together
in stained beauty,
shimmer in sunlight.

The Summer that Wasn't

In Tuscany we sip wine,
walk the countryside,
the vineyard, like crusty bread,
frescoes in churches.
No overflowing bedpans.
No red Popsicles.
No shooting pain.

I'd selected the villa months ago,
because it has a ping-pong table for the girls
and a second level porch to view the stars.
I imagined buying *pesche* with Ana,
eating grapes with Ellery,
sharing a kiss with Paula, my Best, on the terrazzo.
Our first family vacation, the four of us.

But I'm broken and
the three of them, sick.
Ana, sick of folding summer into the Transitional Care Unit.
Ellery, sick of tasting my hospital-pot-pie.
Best, sick of doing it all solo.

My pillows.
My ice packs.
My home.
I readjust my shattered arm, turn on The People's Court.

Best says *we'll cancel.*
I say, *Go without me. You need the break.*

Oxy

I've been awake since the day
I met your incessant silence,
me with deafening dreams.

You are fickle.
So often you go missing.
And always, I collapse with joy
at your return.

Entangled in the line,
I take the bait,
follow your lead, but never get it right.

All my plans, broken.
Weren't we going to Italy?
Didn't I weep to please you?

Another Ambulance Daydream

I was in our kitchen
making sauce, garden tomatoes
simmering in their well of loneliness.

I was dancing barefoot
on the Schooner Hindu,
watching the coast soar by,
playing flute on the quarterdeck.

I know we walked through Provincetown.
I drove.
You flew.
Eggs Benedict at Café Edwige.

I lose myself at the *Song
of Myself* among the intimate
photographs of strangers.

I know I am somewhere
between earth and sky.

Date Night

Best has propped me up in our bed,
I count the peas she's served
in a disposable paper bowl,
the pork chop she's lovingly cut into
bite-size pieces—
I can't manage my own fork and knife.

Best leaves me in the room
with *Forensic Files* reruns,
maybe not love, but loyalty or devotion,
her need for something to be neat,
her need for some shred of order.
The kind we haven't had since
I broke.

The Damned Splint

I turn the dial to increase the angle,
a fraction of misery at a time.
Make it uncomfortable, but not painful,
the splint tells me.
My arm bends to 105 degrees
still has 45 to go.

I do this three times every day,
in the leather chair my mother
bought me at Circle Furniture,
so I could be comfortable. October passes
like the shriveled remnants of morning
glories on our fence. Through the picture

window, tomato vines twist blackish
and limp. And my poor potted hibiscus, confused
with its unseasonable blooms.

7:40 A.M. on a Weekday

First thing this morning,
I'm invisible
just a broken
arm and foot on pillows.
Our daughters slam doors,
dress in mismatched outfits
that I would never let them leave the house wearing.
They holler at each other
Ana, get out of the bathroom!
Ellery's cartoons grow louder and louder—
she's trying to drown out
the clamor of lunch-making.
I hear Coltrane grunt when a spoon hits
the kitchen floor.
Backpacks loaded: lunch-boxes, water bottles.
Time to Go!
Best waves
her hairbrush at everyone,
to get this moving.
A moment later,
everyone is gone, except Coltrane.
There were no goodbyes.

Ode to the Commode

You collect dust in the bathroom—
I haven't used you in a month.
It's an unspoken agreement
between me and your monstrosity.
You will stay there until this whole
thing is over with,
bear witness to
each stabbing shower I take,
until we're sure we don't need
each other
anymore.

The Baltimore Therapeutic Equipment Work Simulator

Each week I visit
the O.T. facility.
I sit at the machine,
grasp the steel wheel,
tilted like a real steering wheel,
pretend to drive,
because I can't, ever since
pain put me
in slow motion.

I'm turning and turning in circles
like my 3-year-old self
at Rye Playland,
a tiny car on a track,
happily spinning,
never really
going anywhere.

Intake Interview: The Ride

Everyone must go in-person to this interview.
To prove that I am truly disabled,
I fold my arm into my sling,
slide one foot into the orthopedic boot,
the other into an old-lady Nike.
MBTA sends The Ride for me—
the driver is a placeholder who grabs my
unbroken arm, steers me into the car, I wince.

Forty-six minutes to get to Charlestown,
each crack and bump in the road
shocks me like smelling salts.
The driver watches as I hobble one-crutched
out of the van and up the handicapped ramp,
careful not to put too much weight on my foot.
I'm trying to cradle my bad arm to avoid being bumped.
Golden Girls rasp in the waiting room.
Strangers stare.

Long fleece sleeves and sweatpants conceal the bruises
up and down my right arm and right leg.
By the time my name is called, I am weary from the Oxy.

How did it happen?
How long will you be unable to drive?
Can you walk down the corridor for me?

Breakdown at CVS

The Ride drops me off,
so I stand here and stare
at the museum case of bottled waters:

Power-C or Triple X?
I'm holding-in my need
to wander aisles—hair notions,

stick deodorants, toothpaste,
every single marked-down seasonal item:

Halloween candy, plastic skeleton, wire witch.

I fumble for my keys
in my coat pocket,
check and recheck

for my iPhone, my keys again,
the spare safety pin I carry in case this very
thing might happen.

Pumpkin-picking Festival: Concord, Mass

I can't go into the patch.
The surface is rippled with rocks,
my gait crutch-uneven,
and I, petrified to trip,
to reinjure, to splinter
and disfigure.

I stand alone,
the air apple-cider-cinnamon-stick,
I don't dare hold my cup one-handed,
shift my weight, ache to stand,
adjust the sling around my arm.

Ana and Ellery weave paths of vines and fruit,
on a hay ride,
roll down the grassy hill,
all tree-line and pumpkin.

I close my eyes.
I shift my weight.
Adjust the sling around my arm.

I Miss My Daughter's First Year of Middle School

Ana's half-looking in the bedroom mirror
and half looking at me, brown eyes narrowing in disgust.
I won't let her leave the house
in a camisole I bought her as underwear.
You're not my mother,
Ana announces,
Rosa is.

Silence.
Scent of her Justice
perfume stings
my eyes.

I hear my own voice:
Well, that was predictable.
Textbook adoptive parent-slash-child conflict.

Ana laughs,
awkwardly and relieved.
She adds a shirt to cover it.
I hobble to my room
to sob.

Four Months Later: I walk again

On my first walk,
a short one,
I pause to consider my
greatest fear—acorns,
hundreds of them, like land mines
beneath my feet.
I tread gingerly.

Atop a pick-up truck
a man showers grass seed
across the berm,
nods to me.

The paddock on Bedford Road contains
the horse, still wearing
a tartan plaid blanket.
His eyes search mine.

In a clear plastic bag,
a sandwich lies
on the sidewalk.
Seems lonely.

I stand at the doorway
to Mrs. Williams' house.
Peek in at her indoor rock garden.
Saint Francis statue stands in ferns,
urges me onward.

Back to Work

Inside my arm,
pain circles round and waits, like
the old green dumpster
in the parking lot.
Teaching reading keeps me
tuned to mind and body,
different now— metallic in places.
My principal offers to carry my books,
asks am I tired, does it hurt?
I am tired. I want slow,
like the subtle growth of plants,
silence after each page turns.

Four Years to the Day

Truth is
I don't
remember her
name, and
heard only
the hiss
of highway
and her
flat metal
voice saying
*I didn't
see her.*

Right of Way

If I could
do it over,
I would
avoid it,
the scene,
the 6-car lot
at the Mobil Station
(Dunkin' Donuts inside).
Skip the stop
for water on
that parched day.
Skip pain, rehab,
a view into life
as an octogenarian,
relearning to function
on the left side.
I'd bypass
the pain.
Revision is not
knowing that for
every trouble-
causer, (the driver)
there are two
do-gooders,
like the sisters
from New Hampshire
who dashed over
to pick up my things,
airborne at impact.
Asked who they could
call for me,
said *it will be OK,*
reminded me to breathe.
The mini-mart manager
fetched ice and water.

EMTs skillfully distracted
me in the ambulance, cracking
jokes about the traffic.
My boss came
to my home, rearranged
the fridge so I could
reach everything easily.
Maybe I could
have done without
the ER doc
who told me *go home*
just before I fainted
from the pain,
but now I have empathy
for medical personnel,
exhausted on inhumane
shifts, unnoticing color
drain from my face
the moment I
tried to stand.
Empathy.
Like how African elephants
grieve and mourn
their dead,
or how my dogs
stood by the crate
of the unwieldy
dog we hosted
in our home
till he could be placed.

With Thanks

I am grateful to Barbara Helfgott Hyett and the PoemWorks community, for sharing the table with me and helping me to be a better poet.

Thanks to Eric Hyett for coaching, editing, and supporting me in completing this project.

I appreciate the support and advice of Shana Hill and Spencer Thurlow.

Thanks to Kristina Watts for her photography skills.

I am thankful for the kindness and expertise of my arm surgeon, Dr. Arthur Christiano.

I will always remain grateful for the extraordinary care of the staff and physical therapists at Emerson Hospital, in Concord, Massachusetts.

Linda Lamenza is a poet and literacy specialist in Massachusetts. Her work is forthcoming or has appeared in *Green Ink Poetry, Lily Poetry Review, San Pedro River Review, The Comstock Review, Nixes Mate Review*, and elsewhere. She is a member of the PoemWorks community in Boston. *Left-Handed Poetry* is her first chapbook.

www.ingramcontent.com/pod-product-compliance
Lightning Source LLC
Chambersburg PA
CBHW030051100426
42734CB00038B/1219